Animal Kingdom Coloring Book is an excellent way for kids to creatively express themselves; Every major animal kingdom or animal type is included. Coloring these wild, mandala-style animals in their natural habitat.

Little rocking flower

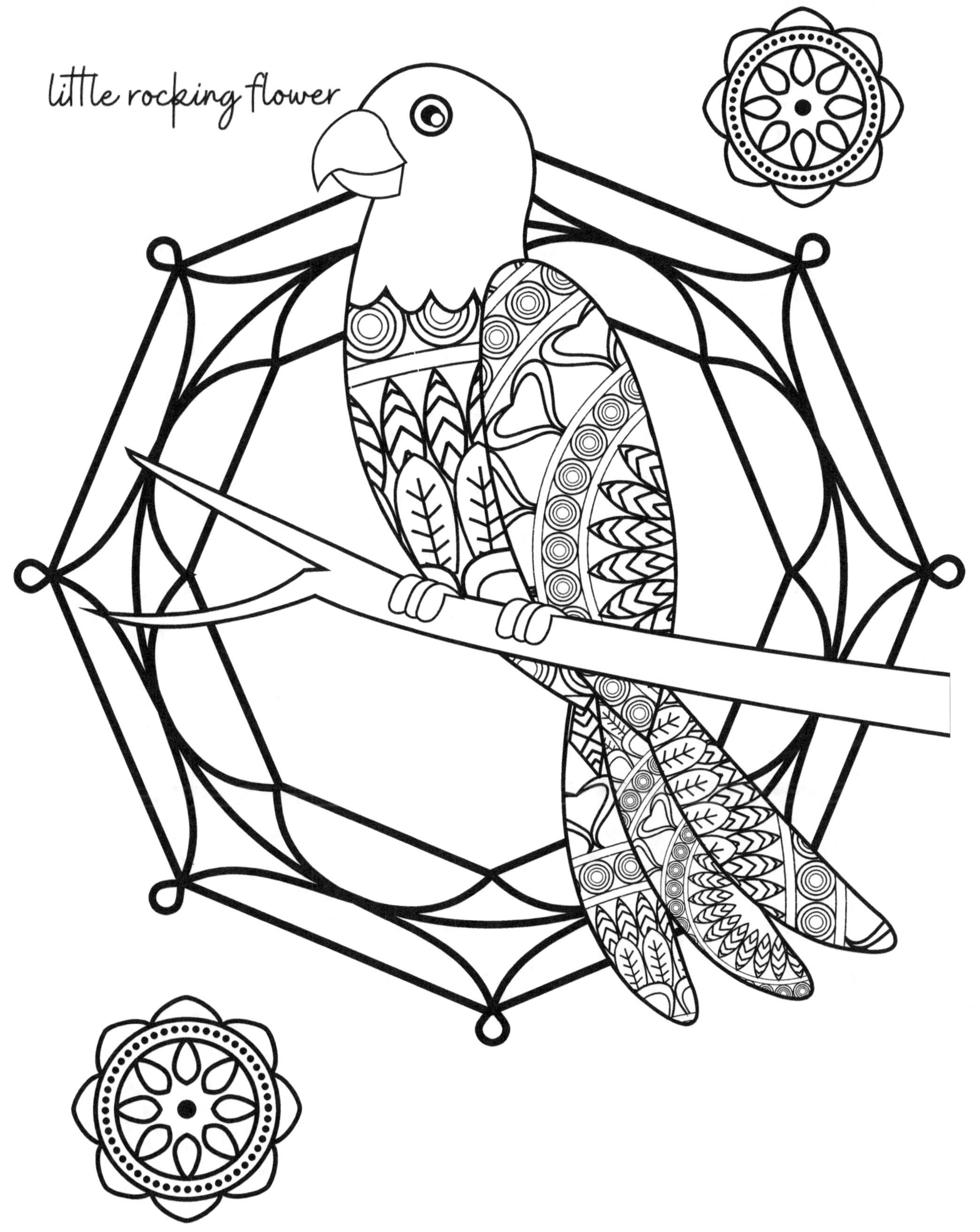
little rocking flower

little rocking flower

little rocking flower

little rocking flower

little rocking flower

little rocking flower

little rocking flower

little rocking flower

little rocking flower

little rocking flower

little rocking flower

little rocking flower

little rocking flower

little rocking flower

little rocking flower

honey

little rocking flower

little rocking flower

little rocking flower

little rocking flower

little rocking flower

little rocking flower

little rocking flower

little rocking flower

little rocking flower

little rocking flower

little rocking flower

little rocking flower

little rocking flower

little rocking flower

little rocking flower

little rocking flower